MW01123179

SUCCESS BASICS

ALOAGBAYE ISRAEL

DEDICATION

This book is dedicated to God Almighty and those who desire success in life.

Table of Contents

ACKNOWLEDGEMENT

I am grateful to my beloved father, Barrister Peter Igietsemhe Momodu, for the sacrifices he made to give my siblings and I the best education he could afford.

I appreciate my sweet mum, Mrs. Roseline Momodu, for her immense support all through the years.

A big shout out to my amazing brothers, Ogie, Kpemi, and Ighemokai for their support.

I appreciate my mentors, Evangelist Queen Omuta, Pastor Kenneth Egede, Pastor Joseph Ibitolu, and Pascal Eruaga for supporting this book project and encouraging me through the years.

To Edirin Edewor, my social media mentor, thanks for the platform you established which helped me connect with great minds to make this book a success. Online Publishers And Entrepreneurs Network (OPEN) is great.

To Eno Sam, my amiable book editor, thanks for your hard work, amazing support and contribution to the success of this book.

God bless you all!

<u>INTRODUCTION</u>

There are a good number of people whose lives are purposeless because they are yet to unveil their potentials. Some others have big dreams but are unable to make those dreams a reality. Are you struggling to be productive? Do your goals seem unreachable? Do you desire to achieve greatness in life? In this book, you'll learn diverse principles of success.

Following these principles helped me graduate at the top of my class with a First Class in Engineering. These practical principles would work for you irrespective of your field of interest. However, the principles in this book will not work for you if you put them in your head alone without applying them to your life. To effectively benefit from the shared basics, strategically follow the action points attached at the end of each chapter.

Have a great read!

THE JOURNEY OF SUCCESS

*D*uring my high school days, I answered English objective questions by guessing. The idea of randomly picking answers earned me low grades because I wasn't working with grammatical principles. I later got an English teacher who taught me that each question had a principle. She emphasized on the need to adhere to the principles in order not to pick the wrong option. For example, a plural noun should be followed by a plural verb. After her thorough tutor, I decided to sit up and apply the numerous principles appropriately in subsequent examinations. In no time, my low grades incredibly turned into distinctions. Of course, this would never have happened if I didn't connect with someone who knew the principles of grammar.

This is exactly how life works. To be successful in life, there are principles you must follow and there are people you should follow. You may succeed temporarily if you live blindly but what sustains true success is a foundation of right principles. Everything in life is built on principles. Mathematical laws are not left out; mathematicians know that once a rule is not applied, the answer to the question will be wrong. Your success in life is dependent on what you do every twenty-four hours. Success is not only a destination to be waited for but a life lived everyday based on principles.

I love the game of chess but I cannot win the game except I know the principles of moving the chess piece. You can't win a chess game by chance except you know the principles of moving each piece. Similarly, before pilots fly planes, they know the predetermined destination and route. If you want to get to a destination, you would probably check Google maps or find a way to know the right route to your destination. Therefore, if your desired destination is success, you must be conversant with the routes. Success principles are the right actions with a predetermined outcome of success. I remember a friend of mine who was to travel to the East from the South back in Nigeria but got trapped. What happened? She had boarded a bus but the driver never knew the route so he drove them around aimlessly. When the passengers noticed that he didn't know the way, they yelled at him as they asked passers-by for the way to their destination. This illustrates what happens when you dream of being successful but you neither know the principles of success nor apply them. I love the way Jesus gave so many principles on the mountain and at the end of it all, he spoke words of wisdom.

Therefore everyone who hears these words of
mine and puts them into practice is like a wise
man who builds his house on the rock. The rain
came down, the streams rose, and the winds
blew and beat against that house; yet it did not
fall because it had its foundation on a rock. But
everyone who hears these words of mine and does
not put them into practice is like a foolish man
who builds his house on sand. - Mathew 7:24-26.

The foolish live by chance but the wise live based on principles. The foolish live for anything hoping that tomorrow would be better but the wise live based on principles knowing that their tomorrow would be a bundle of success. Which category would you prefer?

Knowledge of success principles is good but application of the rules is better.

Knowing the principles of success involves asking the right questions. Below are key questions to ask yourself on your journey to success:

What is my desired future outcome?

What must I do to make my dreams a reality?

When you know what is expected of you and you're willing to do that which is expected of you in every area of life, you are on the right path to success.

To excel in any area of your life, you must ask the right questions and seek the principles. To excel in your education, finance, career, marriage or business, enquire from successful people in that field about the principles they applied which worked for them.

I remember getting off the train on several occasions and unconsciously following others ahead of me with the mindset that we are headed on the same path out of the subway. This didn't work all the time. I have now learnt to always check for the signs on the subway walls or ask for directions. I was heading to my destination by chance which failed me until I decided to follow the principles. To be successful, do not follow the crowd blindly, rather, live by principles. Choose to live every day by principles. In the next chapter you'd understand why this is important in determining what you will become tomorrow.

Action Steps:

List areas of your life where you desire success.

Identify successful people in those areas who you would consider a role model and enquire about the principles they work with.

WE ARE ALL BUILDERS

*T*here's a popular story about an elderly carpenter. He told his contractor about his plans to retire and the contractor asked him to build one more house as a personal favor. The carpenter agreed to do it but this time, the work wasn't from his heart so he used cheap materials and bad workmanship.

After the house was finished, the contractor came by, congratulating the carpenter:

"Here is the key to the front door. This house is my gift to you for your service all through the years "

What a shock! If only he knew that he was building his own house, he would have done it passionately. Well, he had to accept the gift that way; it was no other person's fault but his.

This is how life goes. We are all builders and the way you build your life today will affect your results in the future. Each action you take is a nail, hammer, or brick. Are you building with inferior materials? Remember, this is the only life you will ever build. The irony of life is that most people think they are only having fun when they keep doing wrong things without knowing that they are building their tomorrow. Your results today is dependent on the accumulated choices you made in the past and your results tomorrow will depend on the choices you make today.

During one of the meetings for my induction into the university, our Vice Chancellor gave a sound piece of advice.

"Every word you would write, every class you would attend and every test you would take would count towards your final cumulative grade point average from the university"

This resonated in my heart all through my semesters in school as I decided to give importance to all my academic activities because I earnestly desired to come out in flying colors. All assignments, classes, notebooks and tests were taken seriously as I made constant effort to improve daily. According to Mike Murdock, the secret to your future lies in your daily routine. What do you do hourly? What do you do every day? Whatever you do now, no matter how insignificant you may think it is, will definitely affect your future. If you are a business person and you keep spending your profit for the week or day on unnecessary luxury without saving, you may go bankrupt in years to come. You may likely incur debts beyond your income. Financial carelessness today would lead to an unnecessary burden to bear in the future.

Take the right decisions and develop the right attitude now. Internalize this principle to view your tomorrow through the eyes of your actions today. If you build a bad house, you will get to live in it and if you build a good house, you'll get to live in it but one would definitely be more comfortable than the other. In the next chapter, I would show you two key questions you must answer in order to have a successful life.

The book of your future is not yet written, what would you fill the pages with?

Action Step:

Have a paradigm shift today by daily cultivating good habits and taking the right actions in preparation for a great future.

Read daily
Pray daily
workout
try to eat healthy
Save constantly

IDENTITY AND PURPOSE

*T*o be successful in life, you must discover your purpose and know your identity. Everyone is born with a unique gift which must be unveiled, developed and utilized for productivity. You must discover what you are called to do on earth in order to follow the right course. Many people fail because they pursue what is not meant for them.

If a fish leaves the ocean and tries to climb a tree, it will die in the process. Why? Of course, a fish is destined to swim in water and not to climb a tree. Meanwhile, monkeys can successfully climb a tree but will die if they decide to live in water. This perfectly illustrates the place of purpose.

Often times, people get confused on how to discover their purpose but it is quite simple. If you have issues figuring out who you really are, all you need to do is identify the things you love doing from the depth of your heart for hours without feeling bored even if no one pays you for it. This would give you an idea on what you have passion for. Over the years, what have you been doing joyfully on your own? It could be drawing, fixing electrical appliances, writing, cooking, sewing, speaking or whatever. That is a hint on what you are destined to do and is commonly noticeable at childhood. There is something interesting about discovering purpose; you will perform tasks given to you passionately and efficiently. If someone who loves catering gets a job as a banker, he may feel so frustrated when he is given tedious tasks because he probably took the job only to earn a living and not because he loves the job. To be successful, you must be on your destined path of purpose. When you do your best at what you have passion for, you will be remembered for it.

Having discovered your purpose, you will have to consciously run your dealings with a sense of purpose. This would ensure that everything you do aligns with you fulfilling your purpose. A man does not build a house without a clear purpose in mind. Without a clear purpose, there would be no clear destination and failure would be inevitable. When I was still in school, I knew that my purpose was to get good grades and I worked towards it. Before going into any business, you should know the purpose for starting the business by defining your goals and working towards achieving them.

The knowledge of who you are and what you are born to do makes life more comfortable because your life will be like a square peg in a square hole but a life that is out of purpose is like putting a square peg in a round hole. Of course, this will lead to unproductivity.

However, you need to know your identity after discovering who you are. This implies that you must be definite about your standard and values in life. This will aid you to define the kind of friends you should keep, the type of places you should visit, the kind of books you should read and virtually everything about the life philosophy you should stand for. Never allow people or situations define you, rather, embrace your uniqueness and chase your dreams passionately. It takes a great level of confidence to get to the top. When a fish discovers that its purpose is to swim in water, it will begin to act like a fish and make friends with other aquatic animals. It will have no business with monkeys. You have to be intentional about being successful by eliminating all routes to failure.

God never created anyone a failure but if you refuse to do the needful, you may become a failure. When you discover what you can do from the bottom of your heart even without getting paid, you will be able to serve humanity better with your gifts when you are paid. Everyone has a seed of greatness; everyone has something to offer the world. Just take your time, look within and decide never to leave the world the same way you met it. In the next chapter, you'd understand the place of vision over personal ambitions. True success is not about how much you acquired but how well you understood your purpose to impact the world.

'WHO AM I?' and 'WHY AM I HERE?' are two powerful questions you must answer as you go through life.

Action Steps:

Before you read the next chapter, have a sober reflection on self-discovery.

Write down who you think you are in a diary.

Begin to pursue your purpose passionately.

VISION VERSUS AMBITION

A Danish proverb says,
"Your life is a gift to you from God but what you do
with it is your gift to God".

*V*ision is about what you are willing to give to the world while
ambition is about what you want to get from the world. Your
value in life depends on the value you bring into the lives of
people and nations. Great men are known for the problems they are
able to solve not necessarily the wealth they acquire. To excel in life,
you must be willing to make a difference by leaving a legacy behind.
It is great to be ambitious and probably chase a career but it is greater
to have a vision to touch lives.

Your vision is about your assignment on earth; everyone has solutions to a unique problem in the world. These are signals on the path of your vision:

- those things you are passionate about
- vision could come from those things that frustrate you in your environment
- things you can easily do
- things you would love to do without asking for pay.

A wealthy billionaire was asked,

"How come you still enjoy expanding your business when you already have enough money to take care of your family?"

And he amazingly replied,

"I know that for every new branch I create, I employ another man and that puts food on someone's table and a roof over his head"

This clearly shows his love for serving humanity as he sees the need to give something to the world, thereby, making an impact. You are on your way to success if you don't think about how to acquire wealth alone but about who to inspire. As long as you live, be a channel of blessing to the world by giving them something to remember you for. There is no greater force to achieve success than the force of love.

Right from childhood, my desire has always been to understand how life works and use the lessons learnt to help people. This pushed me to write my first book, 'The Facts Of Life', at the age of eleven. The desire to help people succeed eventually drove me into coming up with 'Success Basics' and I realized it would be selfish to keep the principles shared in this book to myself.

"We make a living by what we get, we make a life
by what we give"
Winston Churchill

Understanding the place of vision over ambition would keep you focused and push you to achieve success. There's another power that differentiates between success and failure which is explained in the next chapter.

Action Steps:

Take a pen now and write down how to want to make an impact in your generation.

Make efforts to act on what you have written.

THE POWER OF YOUR
INNER WILL

hat is the starting point of success? Your environment? The books you've read? What people say about you? The answer to these questions differentiate between success and failure. In recent times, I observed how people act differently even when they are exposed to the same information, situation or success books. While some take up the challenge to succeed, others fail. While some get trapped with life problems, others scale through the same problem successfully. Why can't the useful information exposed to everyone work for everyone? The reason is not far-fetched; success begins with your inner will.

Your inner will is the measure of how strongly you desire to achieve success. Only tough people achieve success because they do not react negatively to the circumstances around them neither do they settle for less than who they are. When your peers or anyone writes you off as a failure, you don't have to settle for that. You must believe in yourself confidently. You must be willing to make your dream a reality irrespective of the obstacles on the way. In chapter four, we addressed the importance of understanding your purpose. Understanding your purpose defines your 'why' power. Your 'why' power would keep you focused and passionate but your 'will' power keeps you determined irrespective of challenges on your success journey. Both of them are very important.

Problems become bouncing grounds when you have an inner will to succeed. I remember how people tried to discourage me back in school by instilling fear in me that it is impossible to graduate with a first class in my department. At a point, I almost fell for their limits but then, my inner will dared to disagree. I decided to put in my very best rather than defining my success by the history in my environment. This taught me that having knowledge without an inner will to succeed is like sitting in a boat without a paddle; you won't move.

Move beyond those boundaries that people or situations create around you. Your only limitation to success are the negative words you accept in your mind. In life, no one can make you fail except you accept failure and no one can bring you down except you decide to remain down. Life would throw lemons at you but you have to decide to turn them into lemonades.

Never forget that your success lies within you and it takes you to become the best of you.

> Champions aren't made in the gym. Champions
> are made from something they have inside of them
> - a desire, a dream, a vision. They have to have the
> skill and the will but the will must be stronger.
> **-Muhammad Ali**

In the next few chapters, you would get to know more principles you must take seriously on the path to success.

Action Steps:

Make a list of areas you desire a positive change.

For each item in 1, write down how you could possibly change from within and activate your inner will in order to achieve your goals.

LEARN GOAL SETTING

*T*he building strata for life are the different goals we set for our lives. Setting goals is an important element in building a foundation for excellence. A basketball game with no goals scored or a football game with no goalpost to score goals would be uninteresting and pointless. Also, when there are no goals to score, life becomes uninteresting and aimless.

Your goals are the little steps you take towards attaining your vision for life. Your vision is your ultimate purpose for life and your goals should be centered around this. Your vision is the big picture while your goals are the little things you should do in order to make that big picture a reality.

Goals create a clear understanding of what lies ahead by preparing you for where you desire to be in the next five or more years. The university system is an excellent way to experience the power of goal setting. During my school days, I set target GPAs for every year. The GPA goals created in me the zeal to study more in order to meet my target. During the first few years, I fell short of my target and re-arranged my GPA goals to meet the final target CGPA which was a First Class.

You need to do the necessary things even though they seem impossible. The reason most people never achieve their goals is that they neither define them nor consider them achievable. It is not enough to set goals verbally because well-written goals show a stronger desire for achievement. I wrote my GPA goals down in school and I kept punching my calculator regularly to be sure I was on track.

"Write down the visions and make it plain on tablets that he may run who reads it" -Hab. 2:2

You would never achieve your full potentials until you set realistic goals capable of creating a strong zeal in you. Your goals would make you grow and increase your capacity to accomplish greater things on your success journey. I deduced a formula for goal setting which I call "The C.A.P Code Of Effective Goal Setting".

The 'C' in CAP stands for 'Clarity'. One important aspect of goal setting is to clearly draw out your goal tags with strategic targets. It will be more effective to precisely put them in writing which will serve as a preliminary guide towards the successful execution of your projects.

The 'A' stands for 'Action Steps' and this involves breaking the clearly stated goals into specific steps by figuring out every 'how', 'what' or 'who' related to your end goal. The action steps should also be clear at each stage such that it will be easier to ascertain if you're making progress or not.

The 'P' stands for 'Purpose'. Taking note of the 'Why' would keep you on track. You need to ask yourself why your set goal is important to you, others or the eventual fulfillment of your life purpose. The answer to this question will keep you motivated to chase your dreams more passionately.

Enough of the theories! Let's practically illustrate "The 'CAP' Code Of Effective Goal Setting". Firstly, you should clearly draw out your goal tags. Assuming you want to save some money at the end of the year, you will have to clearly state the amount you want to save.

Below is a sample:

"By December 2013, I should have saved $1200"

This satisfies the 'Clarity' in 'CAP'.

Secondly, having clearly stated your desired goal, you need to break it into specific action steps by figuring out how the goal will be achieved.

"I will save $100 monthly which is 10 percent of my monthly income of $1000. This would he done via mobile transfer to XYZ Bank"

This clearly states the action steps to be used in achieving the saving goal tag.

Thirdly, you will have to state why you want to save $1200.

"I don't want to borrow during the festive season. I'm saving this to have financial freedom."

This satisfies the 'Purpose' in 'CAP'.

Therefore, the above can be summarized as:

To achieve financial freedom, I have to save $1200 by the end of the year by making a monthly transfer of $100 to XYZ Bank for the next one year.

If you can apply "The 'CAP' Code Of Effective Goal Setting" to your long-term projects, you will successfully execute your projects.

Action Steps:

Apply "The 'CAP' Code Of Effective Goal Setting" to your life projects.

Monitor your progress periodically.

THE THREE "Ds" OF SUCCESS

Walking down the road on a cold snowy morning around Queens Park in Toronto, I saw a homeless guy lying on the road with a police van parked close to him. After few minutes of observation, the policeman drove away. I wondered why the police left him instead of giving him a roof over his head. I soon realized that everyone is given freedom of choice in these societies. They allow you choose the life you want to live even from birth if possible.

Indeed, you are free to choose the life you want to live. Until you consciously make a decision on the life you want and work towards it, life would keep making its unfair choice for you. This is why the first key to open any room of success is 'Decision'.

Becoming successful is a decision and indecision, in itself, is a very costly decision. Some people live without deciding on what they want to get out of life and this is the genesis of failure. Life is a pursuit and you must decide what you want to live for. It is not enough to take life as it comes to you every day; be definite about what you want in life and this would keep your eyes fixed on achieving your goals. A lot of people stand for anything, that's why they are satisfied with anything by relaxing in their comfort zone without any conscious effort. Only wise men become phenomenal because they take the right decisions as at when due. For instance, if you have a project to meet up with and you decide to see movies for hours, your deadline may catch up with you leaving you stranded. It takes a man with inner strength to stay off frivolities when it is time for business.

You are a step ahead if you boldly make the right decisions

It is never enough to make the right decision, how firm can you stand by your decisions? This leads us to the next 'D', 'Determination'. When I decided to graduate from school with the best of grades, I didn't stop there, I became very determined and took my decision seriously. Success does not come by mistake, it comes from a determination to pursue right decisions daily.

Determination is an inner burning desire to be intentional about being successful. When you are determined to get good results, you would stick to your goal tags. Determination is not just about strength but also putting your heart into what you do to achieve your goal. Many people are full of strength but their hearts are carried away by distractions. With determination, your goals will be achievable.

The third 'D' for success is 'Diligence'. Diligence involves hardwork done with discipline consistently. Greatness won't be your portion just because you did a job in the past, rather, a work done consistently with due diligence would surely secure a solid foundation for excellence.

Every true success takes hardwork and discipline

My simple formula for success is:

**DECISION + DETERMINATION +
DILIGENCE = SUCCESS**

Action step:

What do you intend to achieve in life?

Are you clear about this?

Write down your decisions and be determined to follow through diligently.

THE FIVE "Ps" OF SUCCESS

*M*any have big dreams but only few understand what it takes to transform a dream into reality. This chapter unveils five "Ps" for becoming successful. It is essential to understand the pathway to success so that your dreams would not remain mere wishes without actions. Many dreams die because people keep giving excuses and blaming others instead of finding pathways to achieve success. Smart individuals do not stop at dreaming but they take bigger steps to ensure they succeed.

Once you find something you want to succeed in, you are a step into the journey of success. Afterwards, the first 'P' to consider is 'Planning'. Ever wondered why would-be couples usually have a wedding planning committee? Of course, they need to put everything in place before their big day. They need to plan the event and assign duties accordingly and this will help to make the wedding ceremony

THE FIVE "Ps" OF SUCCESS

colorful. I bet you can tell the fate of an unplanned wedding ceremony. If an ordinary wedding of few hours require such planning, how much more your dreams of many years? You should write down all you think you need to do in order to achieve your dream. Planning breeds clarity in achieving vision. Don't just while away time merely talking about your dreams when you should be strategically ruling out your plans on how to ultimately achieve those dreams. The stage of planning is the stage for gathering more information about your dream and should not be joked with.

**Five minutes of planning is better than fifty hours
of mere talk**

The next 'P' in the process is 'Preparation'. Preparation involves stepping out to strictly follow up your plans for vision accomplishment. A plan is a mere write-up if there are no actions backing it up. Some rely on luck to succeed but great men prepare for opportunities. Start preparing now because you can't tell when great opportunities would knock your door. If an employer puts up an advert for applicants to submit their curriculum vitae within one hour, only those who had long prepared theirs would successfully apply. While the unprepared would be wasting time putting an application together, the prepared would have been taken and by that time, the opportunity is gone already. Opportunities will look like a tedious work if you are not prepared. Preparation shows proactivity and this is a key principle for success in any area of life.

**Good luck is preparation meeting with
opportunities while bad luck is lack of
preparation meeting with reality
Eliyahu Goldraat**

Back in school, my goal was to come out tops and I went further to plan my semesters during the holidays. I got prepared by attending every scheduled lecture and reading through past questions against the semester examinations. I learnt something about preparation, it boosts your confidence. Understanding this principle stirred up my confidence in examination halls because I understood that every little thing I did each day was significant towards achieving my goal. How prepared are you for the examinations of life to accomplish your dreams?

The next 'P' to achieve your dream is 'Patience'. Patience is not merely waiting with your arms folded but it is your willingness to keep your eyes fixed on your goal while planning and preparing. There is no such thing as automatic success; sorry to disappoint you. The journey of success is not so rosy but you must appreciate your growth process. Things may seem difficult initially and this is where people get it wrong. They give up when they should be pressing on tenaciously. Success is for people who do not hide their faces when things seem tough. Dreams do not just become a reality overnight. To planning, add preparation and to preparation, add patience and with this, you would understand the process that leads to greatness. While undergoing the third 'P', you may get outrageously inquisitive. How long must I wait? How soon would I achieve my goals? And this leads us to the answer, 'Persistence', which is the next 'P' for success.

Persistence is the key difference between champions and quitters. Champions simply go extra miles

While you patiently go through your growth process, you must be stubbornly persistent about achieving your goals. Persistence is continuously seeking ways to achieve your desired goals. This means that you must be focused and committed to the work required for your dreams to manifest. You need to be flexible with your plan by going back to your drawing board if your goals seem unreachable. Rather than giving up, try figuring out what you did wrong the last time and creatively think of new ways to make it work. It doesn't matter if you plan, prepare or patiently go through your growth process, if you are not persistent, you may end up a failure. Success may come to those who wait but it always comes for those who persist.

The final 'P' which makes the journey of success interesting is 'Passion'. The big question is, how passionate are you about chasing your dreams? Your level of passion for achieving success will determine your level of commitment. If you are passionate about what you do, you will never resort to quitting no matter the storms looking at you in the face. Your passion is the inner strength to withstand every outward pressure. Your passion is the fuel that drives the engine of vision.

**The secret to happiness is not so much in doing
what we like as it is in liking what we do
- Sir James M. Barrie**

A thousand dreams without action is a mere wish; you must wake up to reality and start making moves towards achieving your dreams today. Everyone has an equal chance to achieve success, all you need to do to become extra-ordinary is to put in your best in anything you find yourself doing irrespective of how minor the task could be.

On a final note, possessing the five Ps of success without God is like reading hard for an examination and writing very well during the examination without submitting. Of course, the lecturer will honorably score you below average whether you read hard or not if you do not submit your papers in the examination hall. Most institutions allocate 30% for general tests and 70% for the main exams. It doesn't matter if you score 30%" in your tests, if you don't submit the exam paper of 70%, that will mean you failed.

"For what shall it profit a man if he gains the whole world and loses his soul?" - Mat. 16:26

Do not ignore God on your road to success because your soul is more important than earthly gains.

DREAM ACCOMPLISHMENT EQUATION
PLANNING + PREPARATION + PATIENCE + PERSISTENCE + PASSION= SUCCESS

Action Steps:

Examine your life to find out if you have the five Ps of success. If you lack any 'P', decide now to develop those qualities.

TAKE FULL RESPONSIBILITY

*I*t is vital to take full responsibility for all that happens in your life. Were you unable to achieve your last goal? Take full responsibility instead of blaming the guy next door. You probably failed because you didn't do one thing or the other right. Only failures find every excuse to blame every other thing except themselves and this will make them allergic to success. I recall how students blamed lecturers for their poor grades back in school. Having an F should challenge you to go back to your drawing board. That should motivate you to find out what you did wrong and learn how to do better next time. You have the ability to choose your response irrespective of life's circumstances. This is the power of taking full responsibility.

If you apply for a job and you get no official call-up, you will only be wasting your precious time if you think the employer is hating on you or others are more competent. To take full responsibility, you would have to restructure your resume or learn the required skills for the job. The truth remains that you can't solve any problem by blaming others for it. When you take responsibility for your failure, you create room for improvement.

To further explain the essence of responsibility, I would share something on drug addiction. We get to hear people say that they became the bad people they are because of their messy background. Tales like, " I'm a drug addict because my dad was one" is the lamest of excuses to give for failing in character. What ever happened to you and your place of responsibility? It's obvious that you are a drug addict because you made a choice to be one. Blame no other person not even your parents. You don't have to rot in jail because your dad did too; you should take responsibility to change your life.

If it is to be, it is up to me.
William H. Johnson

You are an individual of your own and you should be in charge of what your life becomes. The world doesn't owe you a living but you owe yourself a lot. Don't be misled into believing that the world owes you a living.

Back in Nigeria, I remember how youths always complained about the hostile nature of the government because they were not offered instant employment after graduation. Most of these youths preferred sitting idle at home to nag daily. In the midst of all these, there were still other young people who got their hands dirty instead of blaming the government. It became obvious to me that the people who take full responsibility for their lives eventually succeed while lazy individuals sleep with failure by blaming others for their failure.

I also remember how I thought my uncle, who was an engineer, would easily provide me a job after my graduation. Unfortunately, he passed on during my third year in school. With this, I understood that I should never give the responsibility for my future to anyone because not everyone would be reliable and not everyone would be around tomorrow. You need a new kind of mentality to succeed and it has to do with being responsible.

**Responsibility comes with power and authority,
when we relinquish responsibility, we give the
power over our lives unto others**

Action Step:

Make a commitment to take 100% responsibility for your failures or success today.

BE POSITIVE

Your thoughts form the most sensitive part of your journey to success. If you must be great, guard your thoughts against negativity. Winners think of great ideas and losers think of excuses. Winners think of everything that could possibly go right while losers think of everything that could possibly go wrong. To take charge of your life, take charge of your thoughts and choose to be on the winning side.

**You can easily know where your life leads by
observing your thoughts**

Your thoughts are so powerful that they can have a magnifying effect on problems. When you focus your thoughts on problems, you would magnify your fear but if you focus on possibilities, your faith will be magnified. Just like a garden is weeded regularly, you need to weed every negative thought disallowing you from believing in yourself.

Your thoughts are the seeds that grow to every other thing that determines how your life goes

It takes discipline to develop positive thoughts and this shouldn't be done in only one day. Controlling your mindset requires mastery developed over time. You can only act based on what you believe and the way you act overtime would gradually become a habit. Since your habits form your character, your destiny will depend on it.

A man who has just lost his job may develop any of these thoughts below:

"I'm really good for nothing. Why is my life so miserable right now? I can't even get a decent job. I may die a jobless man"

"I'm alive and that's a testimony. God still keeps me here for a purpose and there is something in me the world is waiting for. I would get a job soon"

These are negative and positive thoughts respectively. Depending on the way he chooses to think, his life will either remain a mess or turn out to be great. It all begins with your thoughts.

Have you ever noticed that when you think negatively, your mood changes and your face becomes so gloomy? The aftermath of this sick mindset is that your health may be affected due to worry. I quite agree with Corrie Ten Boom who said that worries do not take the sorrows from today but they reduce the strength for tomorrow.

Positive thoughts produce positive confessions which in turn produces powerful energy. Your life transformation begins with your ability to transform your way of thinking. Build your greatness from your thoughts and you would be so amazed at how much you can achieve. Even our greatest guide, the bible, admonishes us to think on only things that are true, honest, just, pure, lovely and of good report.

Action Steps:

Do a thought inventory:

What do you think of the most?

Do you think your kind of thoughts will make you a success or a failure?

If wrong thoughts dominate your mind, write down the right thoughts that would terminate those bad thoughts and develop them daily.

Study this inventory regularly until it becomes part of you.

IS SUCCESS A COMPETITION?

*D*r. Robert Gilbert shared an interesting story about a very famous singer who was invited for a concert in New York. The said singer was to perform with Elvis Presley and many other famous singers but he requested that he should be paid a dollar more than Elvis Presley because he had never beaten him before. His idea of being successful was to earn more than Elvis. He got a dollar paycheck because it turned out Elvis was performing for free. He got the paycheck he requested for but is this really the true definition of success?

Success is not about being better than someone else but getting better at what you do. A competitive spirit breeds jealousy which will definitely blind your eyes to your personal development and progress. The dangers of competing with someone else is that you unconsciously tie your life to a spot because the success of the other person would always get you upset. You would perform below your best if you compete with people below your standard and you would develop inferiority complex or low self-esteem when competing with others who are ahead of you.

What if the lion thinks that producing cow milk is what success is, it would never become the king of the forest. It may end up feeding on mere grass for the rest of its life. You only need to congratulate and learn from those who have achieved success in their own fields. This will save you the headache and inspire you to become a better version of yourself. Success is a personal race and should be seen as such except you want to be limited in life. Limiting your abilities based on what others have achieved would deprive you of excelling in your destined purpose. Do not let history write your story, rather, learn from history and rewrite history with your story. It doesn't matter whether someone else has done it better than you; don't be discouraged because it's not how long it takes you that matters but whether you conquer your own mountain. Some others compare their lives with failures just to have a flimsy excuse to hold onto. This is the height of primitivity and if care is not taken, you may end up worse than those unproductive people you compare yourself with. Activate the genius button in you because your success is very personal.

In my primary school days, we were ranked according to our cumulative scores in all subjects. I came first for three consecutive terms only for a new kid to take my position in a new term. I cried initially knowing that someone had gotten ahead of me but while I walked home, some friends consoled me saying that they even came out lower than me and they weren't crying. I became a bit happy for at least, doing better than most people. I got home to meet my home tutor who made me understand that I was in no competition. He advised me to do better than I did in subsequent terms. This kept me conscious of the principle that success is personal and not a competition.

Action Steps:

Are there people whose success intimidate you?

Do you feel inferior when someone else is becoming very successful?

Do you limit yourself based on other people's failure?

Decide today that the only person you want to compete with is yourself.

THE FUTURE IS NOW

I believe you have dreams and aspirations for the future. Before you got to the point you are today, you may have had some expectations about where you want to be today. Today is the tomorrow you wished for yesterday and your tomorrow would soon be another today. In essence, the future you desire tomorrow begins with your aspirations and actions today.

The future you desire is not waiting somewhere to happen, it begins now. As you hope for a successful future, take the necessary actions today. What do you do daily? What is your daily routine like? Your tomorrow will depend majorly on your answers to these questions. If Mr. A sleeps for a whole day while Mr. B reads and acquires knowledge on how to accomplish his vision for the same period, Mr. A would wake up to remain who he was before he went to bed except he gets a deep revelation in a dream which is most unlikely but Mr. B would become wiser and this will give him an advantage on the journey of success. It is unwise to waste your time on things that do not add value to your life because every minute counts. It takes a deliberate and conscious effort to create the future you desire tomorrow.

Words are easy to say and dreams are easy to describe. Anyone can dream but only few who do the work required within the time frame would eventually achieve success. You may have made mistakes yesterday or realized that you are not where you thought you'd be by today. This could make you afraid of what tomorrow holds but no matter what, yesterday is gone. Tomorrow is yet to come and you can create the future you desire by putting in more effort in today's assignments. Enough of daydreaming and sleeping in the past; take action today because action speaks louder than words. Decide today to take responsibility for what you'd become tomorrow.

Many people are scared of starting small. All they expect is to achieve those big dreams in one day but this is not how it works. Like we earlier learnt, you need to patiently grow through the process. Start from where you are with what you have and be patient enough to start small. Life is like a school where your ability to succeed in one stage will determine if you will be promoted to the next stage. The giant of today was once an embryo who had to grow into an infant and into a teenager before becoming a full grown man. Progressing to the top is a process. Stay put, put in your best and be humble enough till you get to the top. When you get to the top, stay humble!

If the ladder had just one big step to the top, then, nobody would ever climb

In the ultimate book of wisdom, David was humble enough to cater for his father's flocks in the bush when God anointed him to become King of Israel. The secret here is that when you put in your very best to what you do now, you will become a bigger bundle of success tomorrow. Anything worth doing is worth doing well. A man with idle hands is preparing to become a failure in future. Start now!

Action Step:

Make another step today towards achieving the future you desire tomorrow.

ALWAYS SEEK KNOWLEDGE

*I*n the introductory part of the journey of success, I shared a story of my friend whose driver didn't know the route to their destination. They had to look for a way out by asking passers-by about the right way to follow to the East. If they sat in the vehicle without asking for a solution, they would have remained there. Why did I refresh your memory on that story? It is clear that where you are today is as a result of the information you carry. It is what you know that determines how far you go. We are in the information age where access to knowledge is easier than ever before. People do not succeed because they are lucky, they do because they seek knowledge and apply the acquired knowledge to their lives, academics, career or business.

> The illiterates in the 21st Century will not be
> those who cannot read and write but those who
> cannot learn, unlearn and relearn.
> **Alvin Toffler**

Ignorance in itself is not a problem but choosing to remain ignorant is the problem. Your areas of ignorance are only questions that you should seek the right knowledge to answer. Lack of desire to acquire knowledge delays success more than ignorance.

Great readers become great leaders. Develop a reading culture and seek for facts. If you are not loaded with the right information, your head would just be a load with nothing to offload. Success is another word for well-applied knowledge. To stand out from the crowd, you must be knowledgeable. I have always wondered why people do not know how much they can gain from buying a book for the same amount they buy a cup of coffee or soft drink. The nutrient of a meal may last for a little while but the knowledge from a book can last for a lifetime. The knowledge gained from a book is usually priceless compared to the price paid for the book. I love it when Jim Rohn said that poor people have a big TV but rich people have a big book.

Charles Steinmetz, a great electrical engineer was once invited to repair a huge electrical generator in a company's factory. After a few days of research with the generator, its electrical drawings, a paper and a pencil, he walked up to a dynamo and made a large "X" in chalk on the casing. In no time, he gave instructions to the technicians on what to do for the generator to work. Indeed, when they followed the instructions, it worked. The manager was thrilled, and asked him to send an invoice. The bill was for $1,000. The manager got furious and asked him to send his invoice. The manager received the invoice and it contained two items: $1 charge for marking the casing with an X; $999 for knowing where to put it. Indeed he got paid for his knowledge.

What you learn determines what you earn

It is also important that we acquire knowledge that leads to action. It is not enough to know but what you do with what you know is more important. To acquire knowledge without application is like having a house but sleeping on the streets. Your learning should not lead to acquiring knowledge alone, it should push you to take actions.

My favorite book is the bible because it gives great insight to life and principles for purposeful living. The bible gives a foundation for right knowledge. Apply only the right knowledge because in a world of easy access to any kind of information, not every information is useful on the road to success. Read only books that build you up with the right knowledge for a successful life. The book of proverbs is a good place to begin.

> "Buy the truth and do not sell it; also
> wisdom, instruction and insight."
> - Prov.23:23

Action Steps:

Check your goals in different areas of life , career, health, faith, personal development, information technology etc.

Define the knowledge gap you need to fill in these areas.

Develop a book reading plan; one book per week/month.

Buy books of your mentors or role models, read articles online, discuss with people, visit libraries and take advantage of every opportunity to acquire the right knowledge.

HANDLING PEER PRESSURE

*I*f I pick up a football and begin to press it or apply pressure, the ball would only withstand the pressure I apply from outside depending on its internal pressure. If the ball was fully pumped (its internal pressure is high), it would be difficult for me to change its shape by pressing it from outside (increased external pressure) but if the ball was not well pumped (its internal pressure is low), it would be so easy for me to change its shape by external pressure.

Now, picture that scenario and let's relate it to humans; the internal pressure represents your values while the external pressure from outside are peer pressures or pressures from the world. A man of value is not easily influenced by external pressure. This type of man will only be transformed from inside out rather than outside. Your character is an offshoot of your values.

Peer pressure is used to describe the influence on one's decisions by his or her peers. Your peers are probably friends or people in the same age bracket with you. Peer pressure may either have a negative or a positive influence on you. Positive influence could be in form of sports, student politics or voluntary organizations such as Red Cross, Scripture Union, Man o' war or Boys Scouts.

In the world today, we are more connected than ever before due to the revolution of social media. This has made influence from the environment as easy as ABC. Many have taken wrong paths due to negative influence of peer pressure. Some have become kidnappers, armed robbers, sexually immoral, addicts and drunkards all because of negative peer pressure.

"Be not deceived: evil communications corrupt
good manners"
-1 Cor. 15:33

To overcome negative peer pressure, you must develop your own values early in life. Your values are tools to filter external influences. A man without values would fall for anything because if you do not stand for anything, you will fall for everything. You must develop values of sincerity, honesty, focus, purposefulness and love.

If you have defined what you want to be early in
life, then, no one can easily misdirect you.

Friends of similar values move together but a person without values moves with anyone. When you have your values set, a friend who doesn't stand with similar values with you would naturally fall off. For example, you cannot keep a friend who prefers to spend his leisure at a club when you want to be in church. If your internal system is strong, it's either that friend gets transformed or he/she walks away. If you have no values, you may find yourself going to the club with that person. Develop stronger values today, decide what you stand for and choose your friends wisely. True success is not just about making six figures but maintaining good character. To achieve this, do not succumb to peer pressure. For instance, you may be working in an office where everyone dishonestly falsifies figures in order to make some extra cash but they should never influence you. You should report the case instead of joining the band wagon. Your integrity is worth more than a million dollars. Imagine if such people get caught by the Management, they would be fired. Have a strong value system and become a positive influence to the world.

Action Steps:

Write down your value statement today
EXAMPLE:

I choose to love God, love people, shine my light to the world and to positively impact the life of anyone that comes my way.

I choose to maintain my integrity at the office no matter the temptations coming my way.

FAILURE AND MISTAKES

We all have gone through failure at some point in our lives. It is not possible to talk about success without talking about failure and mistakes along life's journey. In the face of failure, some people lose their balance while some others learn from it and develop strength. Which category do you belong to? When we talk about failure, what usually crosses my mind is the story of one of America's best president, Abraham Lincoln. He failed severally before he was finally elected as president. If he had given up at 50 because he failed at 49, he may never have become America's president at 51.

Many people quit so easily when they fail but only a few remain focused even in the face of failure. We forget that failure is a process along the pathway to success. What about Michael Jordan, one of the best players in the history of basketball? Many may feel he never failed but he did. In his words:

> **I've missed more than 9000 shots in my career.**
> **I've lost almost 300 games. 26 times, I've been**
> **trusted to take the game winning shot and missed.**
> **I've failed over and over again in my life. And that**
> **is why I succeed.**

Failure is never failure unless you fail to learn from it. The things you call failure are only experiences. I learnt my greatest lessons in life when I failed at one point or the other but I refused to accept defeat, rather, I thought of better ways to execute the projects. How come? But I failed, didn't I? Could there ever be strength in failure? My dad once told me that cowards die several times but the valiant die only once.

No matter how bad the situation may be, there is still something to learn. There may be an excuse for failing but there are over a hundred reasons you must succeed. There is never a good excuse for giving up because you failed once or twice. The truth is, failure doesn't change your worth, it may just mean that you need to try again with a new method after learning the lessons. Your desire to succeed must supersede your fear for failure.

Never let a bad moment turn into a bad day or a bad day turn into a bad week or a bad week turn into a bad month or a bad month turn into a bad year. Every day is made by God, so be glad and give thanks.

No one ever moves forward by looking backward. What's done is done; the best you can do is learn from it and move to the next level. People who keep looking backwards remain backwards while those who look forward move forward. The future is yet to come, fear not! Learn from your past because all you have is today and you must put in your best to get the best from it. Even after God has forgiven you, you still need to learn to forgive yourself.

If you have never made a mistake, you have never tried anything new

Failure and mistakes should build you up and not break you down. Great men are not those who never made mistakes but those who had enough courage to learn from their mistakes. No matter what you've been through in life, let it bring out your greatest strength for success. The secrets of great men is in their stories of overcoming adversity . So, stand up, dust yourself, take a deep breath and look into your bright future. You must excel!

Action Steps:

Decide to leave the failures of the past today and pick up strength for your success tomorrow.

Identify your past mistakes and learn from them.

CONCLUSION

*D*o you desire success in life? There are many things which can distract you from fulfilling your life purpose. This book is not written to give you knowledge only but to inspire you to take action. You may be the high school student whose dream is to graduate at the top of your class or an entrepreneur who desires business success or a regular person who wants to make a difference in the world. No matter who you are or where you are, I believe in you and you must believe in yourself as well. Remove every form of distraction on your way.

Apply the principles of success you learnt from 'Success Basics' and you would see yourself breaking records in no time. Take the right actions every day in line with your life purpose. Set clear goals with your purpose in mind. Prepare for the future you desire. Never give up on yourself. The journey of success is not a bed of roses so you must take full responsibility for your life. Do not hide under a bushel but bless the world with your uniqueness.

I look forward to reading your success story.

PRINCIPLES OF WEALTH CREATION

*I*f you have read up to this part of this book, you should already know that life is run by principles. The principle of "one plus one equals two" in mathematics remains an eternal truth that nothing can change. This is why I want to share some principles of money or wealth creation which would help you earn more than your random income.

1. PRINCIPLE OF THE MINDSET:

There is no poverty greater than the poverty of the mind. This is why the rich get richer and the poor get poorer. The rich man has developed a mindset to multiply wealth while the poor man is trapped in the poverty of his mind. The poor man sees risk in every opportunity while the rich man sees opportunity in every risk. The poor man can turn one thousand dollars to one dollar while a rich man can turn one thousand to one million dollars. Your mindset must be able to capture and retain wealth for you to prosper.

2. PRINCIPLE OF SOWING AND REAPING:

The principle of sowing and reaping is as old as man himself. It also applies in the area of wealth generation. If you do not know how to sow money when it gets to your hand, money would leave your hands to the person that knows how to sow it. In the bible, the man with one talent lost his talents to the man with ten. You must educate yourself on areas where you can invest and learn how to multiply your money. This principle includes lessons on investment and trading.

3. PRINCIPLE OF VALUE CREATION:

Money comes to those who bring value to the table. The more value you bring, the more money you would earn. This is why you must creatively learn new ways to increase your value. Value involves providing solution to people's problem. As much as possible, identify needs in the society and think of how to satisfy those needs ; this will boost your relevance and create extra income for you.

4. PRINCIPLE OF LONG-TERM PLANNING:

Understanding this principle will make you financially free from weighty debts. Like they say, Rome was not built in a day and little drops of water make an ocean. Do you know how much you'd have to invest if you saved ten percent of your income for the next five years? The problem is, on the short - term, you look at the ten percent as small and squander it because you expect the next pay cheque without any long-term plan. Count the cost and prepare for the future you desire tomorrow. This principle includes lessons on savings and planning. Each time you get your normal income, save at least 10% or 15% of it.

5. PRINCIPLE OF DISCIPLINE:

An undisciplined man cannot be wealthy. Do you squander money? Are you disciplined with your savings? Are you disciplined with your budget? Discipline is an important principle on your journey to financial freedom.

6. PRINCIPLE OF IDEA TRANSFORMATION:

This is similar to the principle of value creation. Value can be created by learning already defined ways of doing things while ideas are created by providing unique ways of doing things; they are unique value adding processes. The poor man always has ideas but never transforms them. This is why you must understand the principle of idea transformation to create wealth. Do not stop at thinking about all the things you would do but get to work before it is too late.

7. PRINCIPLE OF HARD WORK:

I separated discipline from hardwork to show the importance of each aspect in creating wealth. Money does not come to lazy hands. You must be willing to work in order to earn extra income. You may eventually find a way to make passive income without much work but the first entry point requires you work hard. There is no food for a lazy man and taking shortcuts may ruin you.

8. PRINCIPLE OF LOVE

Love works for everything. Just like we earlier compared vision with ambition, you may go far if you have ambition but true wealth comes to those inspired by love for others. True wealth comes to those who are inspired to touch lives. When you have love for people in your heart, you can easily see problems and be inspired to provide solutions to it. You will limit the scope of your abilities for wealth creation if you keep thinking your wealth is only about you.

9. PRINCIPLE OF TIMES AND SEASONS

Ever heard that opportunities comes but once. You must learn to take advantage of the opportunities that come your way. Opportunities are always there but you need to look hard enough and discern the times if you must take advantage of them. Bill gates became a billionaire by taking advantage of lack of desktop computers in homes. In your personal finance too, there are seasons you must learn to save, invest or sow so as to reap enough money in the season of harvest.

10. PRINCIPLE OF EDUCATION

Wealthy people get the required education before going into any venture. They keep growing and investing in their minds in order not to get outdated. In the stock market, for example, those who go there without proper education lose money to those who are properly educated. Get the required education before investing in anything.

ABOUT THE AUTHOR

*A*loagbaye Israel hails from Edo state, Nigeria. He is the convener of 'The Pathway to Destiny' at God's Covenant Ministries, a programme geared towards equipping youths to be relevant in the 21st Century and fulfill God's purpose for their lives. He is also the director of programmes with 'World Reformers Initiative', a non-governmental organization in Nigeria created to impact the world through humanitarian gestures and inspirational messages. He is currently on study leave from his position as a lecturer at the University of Benin, Department of Production Engineering. He is a PhD candidate at the Department of Mechanical and Industrial Engineering, University of Toronto, Canada and has continuously volunteered to impact lives at his local church, Redeemed Christian Church of God, Jesus House.

CONNECT WITH ME:

Thank you for buying and reading this book. Please leave your reviews and connect with me on my blog and social media platforms:

Website : www.inkspirednow.com

E-mail: aloagbaye@inkspirednow.com

Instagram: @dkingisrael

Facebook page: facebook.com/inkspirednow

You can also join my Facebook group, 'Wealth and Value Creation Network', to connect with other great minds.

Facebook Group: Facebook.com/groups/wavcn

To your success,

Aloagbaye.

Made in the USA
Middletown, DE
21 August 2019